NIFTY
FIFTY

D1616639

NIFTY FIFTY

ISBN 0-936110-06-6
Library of Congress Catalog Card Number: 87-051619
Copyright 1988 by Greta Rasmussen
All rights reserved. Printed in the U.S.A.
10 9 8 7 6 5 4 3

TIN MAN PRESS
BOX 219
STANWOOD, WA 98292

Contents

Introduction

What we hope you will be dealing with in "Nifty Fifty" is the "Aha!" factor — that wonderful sense of intellectual excitement we experience when ideas snap into focus or when something occurs to us for the first time.

"Nifty Fifty" attempts to bring this "Aha!" factor into play by asking fundamental, provocative questions about fifty very ordinary things — things as plain as apples, cookies, bowls and birds. (No aardvarks or abacuses here!) Why such simplicity? Because children, like adults, care most about things that touch their lives in some direct, meaningful way. As a result, there are many more motivational possibilities — and, therefore, more "Aha!" possibilities — in everyday things than there are in exotic things. "Nifty Fifty's" premise is as simple (and as profound) as that.

Those of you who know our DISCOVER! card set series will not be surprised by the everyday nature of our subjects. However, there is one fundamental difference between DISCOVER! and "Nifty Fifty." While DISCOVER! is hands-on, using the actual object as the starting point for the activities, which are often observational in nature, "Nifty Fifty" inquiries are almost totally conceptual. In other words, the purpose here is not to ask a child about one particular sock, but rather (with apologies to Plato) about "sock-ness."

You can probably make best use of "Nifty Fifty" in your classroom by presenting the questions orally, handling one subject area at a time. Let children discuss each question as fully as they can, and by all means, encourage any creative meandering that takes place as they attempt to formulate their answers.

While we're on the subject of answers, it should be noted that we have not attempted to give you all of the possible responses, but rather to provide the best (and most succinct) answer that has occurred to us. If one of your bright students comes up with something we have not anticipated, we say…"Bravo!" Or, rather …"Aha!" You may well find that other "spin-off" possibilities will occur to you as you and your students toss ideas around. If so… "Aha!" again.

Finally, we hope this book will make a small contribution toward the goal of helping children improve their thinking abilities. We hope it will sensitize, sharpen, and make them more aware. We hope it will provide some insights into the process of critical and creative thinking. To this end, we have done our best to make certain that the questions can be answered without relying too heavily on prior knowledge. Obviously, this is not totally possible, but at least we have tried.

For all its apparent simplicity, "Nifty Fifty" has given us here at Tin Man Press a real intellectual workout, if for no other reason than the fact that when you are talking to a child about sticks, grass or pets, your thinking had better be on the mark! We hope you and your students will have as much fun with this book as we have had.

GROCERY STORE

1. If you couldn't read, could you still shop in a grocery store? Discuss.

Yes, but you would miss a lot of information, such as brand names, contents of boxes and cans without pictures on the labels, etc.

2. Why do grocery stores keep the same kinds of groceries in the same place all of the time?

So that people who shop at the same grocery store all of the time will know where to find things.

3. Why would the manager of a grocery store have to buy lettuce more often than soup?

Because soup can be preserved in cans, but lettuce is good only when it is fresh.

4. Why do you think there are more brands of breakfast cereal than brands of salt?

Because people want salt to be the same every time they buy it. People like many different kinds of breakfast cereal.

5. Why do the aisles in grocery stores have to be as wide as they are?

So there is room to shop comfortably and so that two grocery carts can pass easily.

6. The aisles in grocery stores are usually numbered. Why?

To make it easier to find things.

7. The checkout counter where you pay is always near the front of the store. Why?

To make it easy to get groceries from the store to the street or parking lot, and to make sure people pay for their groceries.

8. If you bought four cans of vegetables, a dozen eggs, and a loaf of bread, which would the checker put into your bag first? Why?

The cans of vegetables. Since they are heaviest, they would go in first to make sure they didn't break the eggs or squash the bread.

9. Most grocery stores put their biggest ads in Thursday newspapers. Can you figure out why?

Because most people do a lot of their grocery shopping on the weekend and Thursday ads give them time to make their shopping lists.

10. People probably shop in grocery stores more often than in any other store. What are three other stores people use a lot?

Discount store, drugstore, convenience store, etc.

STAIRS

1. In one sentence, explain the main purpose of stairs.

Stairs help us to get from one level to another.

2. What determines the size of a step...
— from front to back?
— from side to side?

Front to back — the size of our feet; side to side — the width of our bodies.

3. Why are people usually more careful going down stairs than going up stairs?

Because if you fall going down stairs, it is very hard to stop yourself.

4. Why are all the steps in a set of stairs always the same height?

So that every step we take will be the same and we won't trip.

5. In every two-story house, there are usually the same number of stairs. Why?

Because most rooms, and therefore most staircases, are the same height.

6. Besides stairs, what other ways do people have to get from one level of a home or building to another?

Elevators, escalators, maybe ladders. (Firemen sometimes use poles.)

7. Why don't you find stairs in a supermarket?

Because if there were stairs, people couldn't use grocery carts.

8. Tall buildings usually have elevators, but they also have stairs. Why?

Sometimes elevators don't work, so stairs are also needed.

9. Why aren't kitchens usually on the second floor of a house?

Because so many things are carried into and out of the kitchen that it wouldn't be handy.

10. In a seven-story building, how many regular sets of stairs would there be?

Six.

BREAD

1. **What is your favorite kind of bread and why?**

   Answers will vary.

2. **A slice of bread usually has a dark crust around it. Why is that?**

   Because when bread is baked in an oven, the outside part is exposed more directly to the heat source and gets brown.

3. **Why do people usually cut bread so it is flat before they eat it?**

   Because things such as butter and jam can be spread more evenly on slices of bread than on chunks of bread. Also, sliced bread is better for sandwich-making.

4. **Can you name three reasons why bread comes in wrappers?**

   To keep it from getting stale; to keep it clean; and to give information such as brand, type of bread, etc.

5. **About how many bites do you think are in one slice of bread? If there are 20 slices in a loaf, how many bites would that be?**

   Answers will vary, but probably nine or ten bites; and therefore, 180 or 200 bites in a loaf.

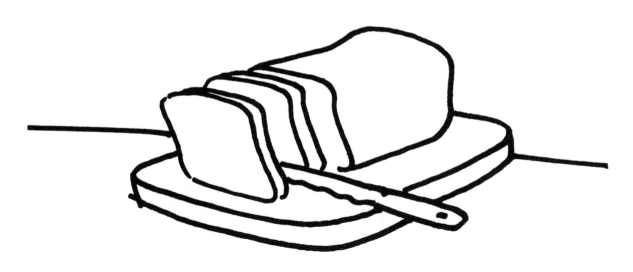

6. **If you wanted to bite a hole in the center of a piece of bread, what would be the best way to do it?**

Fold the bread and take a bite from the middle.

7. **Why do people sometimes prefer toast to bread?**

Because people sometimes like warm foods. Toast will also melt butter, and it has a crispy texture.

8. **If you rolled a slice of bread into a ball, do you think the ball would be about the size of a basketball, baseball, or ping pong ball?**

A ping pong ball.

9. **Why do loaves of bread always seem to be about the same size? They can be round or rectangular, but you never see loaves which are really huge. Why do you think that is?**

They would be hard to bake and would probably get stale before they were eaten.

10. **Think of one way bread is used at breakfast, at lunch, and at dinner. Make all your answers different.**

Breakfast — toast; lunch — sandwich; dinner — untoasted with butter.

TELEPHONE

1. **This sounds like a silly question, but answer it seriously. Why can't a one-year-old baby use a telephone?**

   Because a one-year-old baby can't talk, can't dial, and would have trouble holding the phone.

2. **Why don't classrooms in schools have telephones?**

   Too disruptive.

3. **Telephone messages in cities and towns are carried on wires outside your house. Why are the wires placed on high poles?**

   Chiefly to protect the wires and keep them out of the way.

4. **Why do you say "hello" when you answer the phone? Why not just pick up the receiver and wait for someone on the other end to say something?**

   You have to say "hello" first so that the caller knows you are on the line.

5. **The part of the telephone you hold is always about eight inches long. Why?**

   That is about the average distance from the ear to the mouth of an adult.

6. **Why doesn't a telephone have just a flashing light to let you know when someone is calling?**

   Because you might not be looking at the phone when someone is trying to call you.

7. **Who would use a telephone most often — a cashier at the supermarket, a nurse, or a secretary?**

   Probably a secretary.

8. **Why are people's last names always listed first in telephone directories?**

   Because many people have the same first names and not as many people have the same last names.

9. **Why is it important to put people's addresses in phone books?**

   To provide additional help in telling people apart.

10. **You usually have your own telephone number memorized. What other numbers or facts about your own life do you have memorized?**

    Street address, birth date, etc.

BANDAGE

1. **A bandage is made of tape, with a cotton (gauze) part in the center. Why can't it be all tape?**

   Because tape would hurt the wounded place.

2. **Why is there almost always more tape than cotton in a bandage?**

   So the bandage will stay in place.

3. **Why do bandages come in different sizes?**

   Because wounds have different sizes and shapes. Also, various parts of our bodies are shaped differently.

4. **When you buy a box of bandages at the store, each bandage is wrapped in paper. Why?**

   To keep the bandage clean and germ-free.

5. **Do you think children or adults use more bandages? Why?**

   Children, because they are more active and get more cuts and scratches.

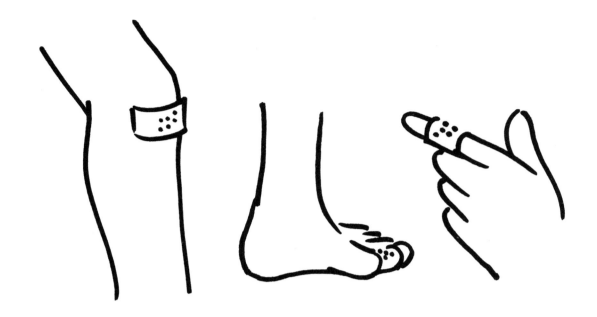

6. Why don't you put a bandage on a black and blue mark?

It would not help, since the skin is not broken.

7. Why is it easier to keep a bandage stuck to your forearm than to your elbow?

Because your elbow bends and your forearm doesn't.

8. Why would it hurt more to take a bandage off your arm than off your finger?

Because there is more hair on your arm.

9. Do you think you use more bandages in the winter or summer? Why?

Probably during the summer, because more time is spent playing outside.

10. When you take a bandage off, should you yank it or take it off slowly?

Answers will vary.

BOWL

1. A bowl is a little bit like a spoon. How?

It is shaped so that it can hold liquid.

2. Name some foods you usually put in a bowl.

Soup, chili, cereal, pudding, ice cream, applesauce, etc.

3. Can you think of a good reason bowls aren't square?

Hard to wash, hard to store, hard to get that last spoonful.

4. If you put the same amount of hot soup in a bowl and in a cup, and both the bowl and the cup were the same thickness, which would keep the soup hot longer? Why?

The cup, because a smaller amount of the soup would come into contact with the air.

5. Why is food for dogs and cats usually put in bowls rather than on plates?

So that it won't be scattered around when the animal eats.

6. If you had two bowls the same size and you filled one with water and the other with popcorn, which would be heavier? Why?

The bowl filled with water, because popcorn is lighter than water and there would be many air spaces between the pieces of popcorn.

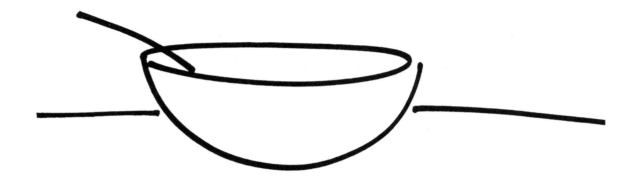

7. **Think of the way a bowl looks when it is upside down. Name something like an upside-down bowl that...**
   — is alive.
   — you can climb.
   — people live in.

   Alive — turtle, ladybug; can climb — hill (also, some playground climbing equipment is dome-shaped); people live in — igloo, some tents.

8. **If you could use only a bowl or a plate to eat with for the rest of your life, which would you choose? Why?**

   Probably a bowl, because a bowl will hold both solids and liquids.

9. **Think of a bowl filled all the way to the top with milk. Would there be more milk in the top half or the bottom half? Why?**

   The top half, because it is bigger.

10. **Bowls do not have handles. What other things found on a dinner table do not have handles?**

    Plates, glasses, napkins, most salt and pepper shakers, saucers, tablecloth.

FARM

1. Why don't you find big farms in the middle of a city?

Because there isn't enough room. (The land in big cities costs too much.)

2. Why are some farms larger than other farms?

Because some farmers have more money than others and can afford more land. Also, some crops need more land than others (for example, a wheat farmer needs a lot more land than a lettuce farmer.)

3. Why are barns so big?

Because barns hold big things, like tractors. Some barns also have space for animals and for hay.

4. Who would probably be more interested in a weather report — a farmer who grows corn or a farmer who keeps dairy cattle? Why?

Probably a farmer who grows corn, because corn needs rain at certain times. (Food for dairy cattle is stored for fairly long periods. Therefore, weather on a day-to-day basis isn't as important.)

5. There is often a row of tall trees on one side of a farmhouse. Why do you think trees are planted there?

To protect the farmhouse from wind.

6. Why are many crops a farmer grows planted in rows?

Because they are easier to plant, to take care of, and to harvest.

7. Why do many farmers take vacations in the winter?

Because they are busy with their crops in the summer.

8. How do farmers make money?

They sell the things they grow and the animals they raise. Also, dairy farmers sell milk, sheep herders sell wool, etc.

9. What might be some of the hardest things about being a farmer? What would be some of the best things?

Hardest — getting up early, hard work, weather problems, animal illness; best — outdoor work, young animals, knowing that your work helps feed people, being your own boss.

10. Farm is a one-syllable word. Think of all the words having something to do with farms which have one syllable. Think of animals and think of crops. Oops! There's one: crops!

Barn, fence, horse, cow, lamb, straw, corn, plow, seed, wheat, pig, shed, hay.

BALL

1. **Some balls bounce, but all balls can do something else. What?**

   They can roll.

2. **What happens if you bounce a ball which has the air partly out of it?**

   It doesn't bounce very well.

3. **If you started a baseball and an apple rolling down a hill at the same time, which would probably get to the bottom first? Why?**

   The baseball, because it is more round than the apple.

4. **What ball used in a game is...**
   — about the size of a penny?
   — about the size of an orange?
   — about the size of a pizza?

   Penny — marble; orange — baseball, tennis ball; pizza — basketball, volleyball.

5. **Do you think there are more lost baseballs or basketballs? Why?**

   Baseballs, because baseballs are smaller than basketballs. Also, there are more places to lose a baseball in areas where baseball is played (outside in large fields) than there are in places where basketball is played (gyms or playgrounds.)

6. **Think of a ball that...**
   — **is sweet and comes out of a machine.**
   — **breaks apart when you throw it.**
   — **has holes in it.**

   Sweet — jawbreaker or gum; breaks apart — snowball; holes — bowling ball.

7. **Some long skinny things like string or yarn are kept rolled in a ball. Why?**

   Because it keeps them from getting tangled and makes them easy to store.

8. **Think of sports and all the things used to make a ball move in games. What are some? Here's a start: baseball bat.**

   Hand, foot, tennis racket, pool cue, field hockey stick, table tennis paddle, golf club.

9. **When you throw a ball, what determines how far the ball will go?**

   How hard you throw it; the size and weight of the ball; whether there is any wind.

10. **What is the biggest ball you can think of?**

    Answers will vary, but "the sun" is probably a good response.

SIGN

1. Where do you see more signs — in the country or in the city?

In the city.

2. Why are most signs up high?

So that they can be seen more easily.

3. Why do most road signs have words or pictures on the front and not on the back?

Because they are usually seen by people moving in one direction.

4. Why do you see a lot of advertising signs on the main streets of cities and towns and almost none along streets in neighborhoods?

Because there are more people to see the advertisements on the main streets. Also, most home owners wouldn't want signs in their yards.

5. Why do most signs have large letters?

So they can be read from a distance.

6. **Why do most signs have very few words?**

   Because signs are designed to give simple messages which can be read quickly.

7. **If you couldn't read, which signs would mean more — road signs or advertising signs?**

   Road signs, because they are always shaped the same and they often use symbols.

8. **What kind of sign do you find on almost all houses and stores in cities and towns?**

   Street address signs.

9. **Why don't stop signs come in different colors and shapes?**

   Relates to question 7. So that they are easily recognizable.

10. **If you had to make a sign about a circus coming to town, what would you want the sign to say?**

    Name of circus, show dates and times, where it will be, price of admission, featured acts.

BOOK

1. Name three places or buildings where you would find a lot of books.

Schools, libraries, bookstores.

2. Continue this series: book, chapter, page, paragraph...

Sentence, word, letter.

3. Why are book pages numbered?

So that we can use an index. Also so we can find certain parts of a book easily.

4. Why don't the words in a book completely cover each page?

Just as a school day without recess would not be any fun, so a page without margins or spaces would not be fun to read.

5. Explain the main differences between a magazine and a book.

A magazine is published every month or so and is usually thrown away. A book comes out only once and is usually kept for a long time.

6. Why is the paper in books usually white?

So that the words will show up clearly.

7. Why don't we open books and start reading just anywhere?

Because most books have a beginning, a middle, and an end, with one idea leading to another.

8. Can you think of a book which might have your last name in it?

The telephone book.

9. What kind of book might you find...
   — in the kitchen?
   — in a schoolroom?
   — in a living room?

Kitchen — cookbook; schoolroom — textbook, workbook; living room — a book with stories, a book with pictures, a novel.

10. In your opinion, what are the three most common words found in any book?

Answers will vary. A, the, and, an, of, in — all are good responses.

ICE

1. What is ice?

Frozen water.

2. What time of the year do people use the most ice cubes?

In the summer.

3. Which would melt first at room temperature — a 100-pound block of ice or 100 pounds of ice cubes? Can you say why?

100 pounds of ice cubes, because there would be much more surface touching the warmer air.

4. Besides ice, what other kinds of frozen water can you see in the winter?

Snow, sleet, frost, hail.

5. Would you rather fall down on snow or on ice? Why?

Probably snow. It is softer than ice.

6. Why do icicles always hang down?

Because they are formed by dripping water, and water runs downhill.

7. **If you had two ice cubes and you put one of them on a table and held one of them in your hand, which would probably melt first? Why?**

   The one in your hand, because your hand is usually warmer than a table or the air in a room.

8. **Which could walk on ice more easily — a horse, a cow or a dog? Why?**

   A dog, because it has pads on its feet, not hard hooves.

9. **How do you suppose people got ice before there were refrigerators?**

   They cut ice from frozen lakes and rivers during the winter. (They stored it in straw or sawdust in special ice houses to make it last as long as possible.)

10. **What is the most important thing you need to know before you go skating on a frozen lake?**

    The thickness of the ice.

EAR

1. Why do we have two ears?

We have two ears so that it is easier for us to hear sounds coming from different directions.

2. Why do our ears stick out from our heads in a cupped shape?

To help us catch sounds (or sound waves).

3. Why are our ears usually the first thing to get cold on a winter day?

Because they are thin and stick out from our body. Also, they are often not covered up.

4. Some animals have ears that can actually move in the direction of sounds. Since our ears don't move very much, what do we do?

We turn our heads.

5. What is the loudest sound you have heard today?

Answers will vary.

6. There are only two possible ways to see your own ears. Can you name them?

In a mirror or in a photo.

7. **"Ear" is a one-syllable word. How many other things that are part of your head have just one syllable? Here's a start: chin. Can you name at least six?**

Nose, skin, eye, lash, teeth, lips, tongue, gum, jaw, cheek, brow.

8. **Why do you think a hippopotamus has ears that are close to the top of its head?**

So a hippo can have its head almost completely under water and still have its ears above the water.

9. **Why do rabbits have bigger ears than lions?**

Rabbits need to hear very well so they can run away from their enemies. Lions have no natural enemies, so they do not need such big ears.

10. **What is the very first sound you usually hear in the morning and the very last sound you usually hear at night?**

Answers will vary.

WINDOW

1. Why do people put windows in walls?

For light, ventilation, to be able to see outside, and because they look nice.

2. Why are most windows squares and rectangles and not circles or other shapes?

Because it is easier to open and close them, and easier to build them into walls.

3. Why can't whole walls be made of glass?

They wouldn't be strong enough. Also, they wouldn't provide privacy and would be too cold or too hot.

4. Why aren't windows put down low near the floor?

Because it would be hard for us to see out. Also, they could be broken easily, and the light they let in would not fill the room very well.

5. Why don't dog houses have windows? Why don't most sheds have windows?

A dog house, like a den, gives warmth and security. Therefore, a dog would not like a house with windows. Since people don't spend much time in sheds, windows aren't needed.

6. Why shouldn't we just forget about doors and come through windows instead?

It would not be convenient. Also, some windows would be too small or too high up.

7. Which would probably have the largest windows — a movie theater, a supermarket, or a doctor's office?

A supermarket.

8. Why do most stores have windows only in the front?

Stores need the other walls for shelves and displays. For security also.

9. Think of two things people use to cover their windows. Think of three reasons why they cover them.

Blinds, shades, curtains, drapes, shutters, etc. They are covered for: privacy, to darken a room, to keep a room cooler or warmer, to look nice.

10. Besides windows, what other things in a house are always made of glass?

Mirrors, light bulbs, certain light shades or coverings, drinking glasses, jars.

BRIDGE

1. **Why do we need bridges?**

   So we can cross things that are in our way.

2. **What is the most common thing that bridges cross? What other things do they cross?**

   Rivers (or streams) is probably the best answer. Bridges also cross roads, railroad tracks, lakes, bays, etc.

3. **When a bridge crosses a river, why is it usually fairly high above the water?**

   To keep it safe from floods; to allow boats to pass beneath.

4. **How is a tunnel something like a bridge?**

   It helps us past an obstacle.

5. **How do you think people first got the idea for a bridge?**

   Answers will vary — possibly a fallen log across a small stream.

6. **What would be some of the biggest problems in building a bridge all the way across the ocean?**

   Depth of water, currents, storms, distance.

7. **In the winter, the surface of a bridge often freezes before the rest of the road. Why do you think this happens?**

   The bridge surface is not insulated by the ground; it is completely surrounded by the cold air.

8. **Do you think there are more rivers or bridges? Why?**

   Bridges, because almost all rivers are crossed by more than one bridge.

9. **If you put two books a few inches apart on top of a table, what things in your house could you use to make a bridge between the books?**

   A ruler, pencil, other books, etc.

10. **Why aren't there ever stoplights in the middle of bridges?**

    Because there are no intersections.

HOUSE

1. Name at least five soft things you would find inside a house.

Pillows, rugs, blankets, towels, paper towels, paper tissue, sponges, powder puffs, chair and sofa cushions, beds.

2. Name at least eight metal things you would find inside a house.

Pots, pans, pipes, tools, utensils, stove, refrigerator, bed frames, door knobs, coat hangers, hinges, locks, nails, screws.

3. What are some of the materials used to cover the outside of houses?

Wood, brick, stucco, shingles, stone, concrete, plastic or metal siding.

4. Why do houses have rooms?

To provide privacy and separate spaces to do different things.

5. Name the different kinds of rooms found in almost all houses.

Living room, bedroom, kitchen, bathroom, dining room.

6. In which room do people spend most of their time standing up?

The kitchen.

7. A floor is important in a house, but there are two things even more important than a floor. What are they?

Wall, roof.

8. Why do houses face the same direction on a city block?

Because it is handy to have the front door face the street. Also, the block wouldn't look nice if houses faced in all sorts of directions.

9. Could a tent be called a house? Why or why not?

It depends. Most people think of a house as something permanent. If you lived in a tent all the time, it could probably be called a house.

10. What room do you like best in your house? Tell why.

Answers will vary.

TREE

1. What is the strongest part of a tree?

The trunk.

2. What are some of the reasons why trees fall down?

Wind, disease, floods, people cutting them down.

3. Name as many parts of a tree as you can.

Root, bark, trunk, branch, twig, leaf, bud, sap, etc.

4. Think of two reasons why people plant trees in their yards.

For shade, to look nice, for fruit or nuts. (Also as a windbreak.)

5. Why are some trees easier to climb than others?

Some trees have a lot of evenly spaced branches that grow out from the trunk.

6. What is the difference between a log and a board?

A log is just part of a tree trunk; a board has been cut with a saw so it is smooth and straight.

7. Trees are tall. Buildings are tall. Which is taller — the tallest tree or the tallest building?

The tallest building. (Tallest building (1987), Sears Tower, Chicago, 1454 ft.; tallest tree (1987), in U.S., California Coast Redwood, 362 ft.)

8. Why are trees hard to draw?

Because they have so many branches, leaves, twigs, etc.

9. Which season of the year would it probably be if the leaves were...
   — orange?
   — light green?
   — dark green?
   — gone?

Orange — fall; light green — spring; dark green — summer; gone — winter.

10. Name everything in the room where you are now that comes from a tree.

Pencil, desk, paper, ruler, picture frame, etc.

BATHTUB

1. Why can't you float in a bathtub?

The water isn't deep enough.

2. If you filled a bathtub all the way up to the top edge and then got in, what would happen? Why?

The water would run over, because there wouldn't be room for all of the water and for your body.

3. Why is the bottom of a bathtub slanted slightly?

So all of the water will run out when you open the drain.

4. Which would be more fun to play with in a bathtub — three rocks, three pieces of wood, or three buttons? Explain.

You probably could have more fun with the three pieces of wood, because they would float.

5. Why do people always sit the same direction in a bathtub?

Because they want to face the faucets.

6. Why aren't bathtubs made out of wood?

Wood would not last very long and it would be hard to clean. You might also get splinters.

7. Why are the top edges of bathtubs usually flat?

So there will be a handy place to put things such as soap, shampoo, etc.

8. Why are bathtubs usually rectangular rather than circular or oval?

Our bodies fit well into a rectangular shape. Also, a rectangle is easy to fit into a corner or against a wall.

9. Which of the following things is least like a bathtub, and why? A bowl, a drawer, a lake, a lamp shade, wastebasket, a box.

A lamp shade, because it is the only thing that doesn't hold something.

10. If you had a piece of cake and a slice of bread floating in a bathtub, which would fall apart first? Why?

Probably the piece of cake, because it would crumble more easily than a piece of bread.

MEAL

1. Why don't we eat a little bit all day long, whenever we feel like it, rather than eating most of our food in the form of meals?

Because we probably wouldn't get a balanced diet, and it would sometimes get in the way of other activities.

2. Why don't we usually eat as much for breakfast as we do for dinner?

Because we have just been asleep and we aren't very hungry.

3. Can an apple and a bowl of popcorn be called a meal? Why or why not?

No, because a meal usually contains several things that are good for us, such as fruit, vegetables and meat.

4. Meals are sometimes served in courses. If the first course is soup and the third course is pie, what might be served for the second course?

Meat and a vegetable, spaghetti, chicken and rice, etc.

5. Think back to the meal you ate five meals ago. What was it?

Answers will vary.

6. What foods might you eat in the summer that you probably wouldn't eat in the winter?

Watermelon, cantelope, barbequed hamburgers, potato salad, snow cones, etc.

7. Why don't people usually eat pancakes and french fries during the same meal?

Because pancakes are usually eaten for breakfast and french fries are eaten for lunch or dinner. Also, they are both quite filling and probably wouldn't taste very good together.

8. Why are the meals served at school the same, or just about the same, for everybody?

Because it would be too hard to make many different kinds of meals.

9. Farmers often eat their biggest meal at noon rather than in the evening. Can you think of a reason why?

Because farmers get up very early and work hard in the morning, and they are hungry by noon.

10. Name some advantages of eating your meal at a table.

You are less likely to spill; it is easier to reach things like salt and pepper, ketchup, etc.; it is easier to have conversations with other people.

STICK

1. **What is a stick, really?**

   Part of a tree branch.

2. **In what month do you think you would see the most sticks on the ground?**

   Probably March or April (because of wind).

3. **Where would you probably find the most sticks and the fewest sticks...**
   — **in a park?**
   — **in a yard?**
   — **on a ball field?**
   — **on a street?**

   Most — in a park; fewest — on a ball field.

4. **If a stick had a leaf on it, what would that say about the stick?**

   It has recently been alive.

5. **Which would be easier to bend — a stick that has just come off a tree or a stick that has been on the ground a long time?**

   A stick which has just come off a tree, because it would have more moisture in it.

6. **Which of these two words would be easier to make out of sticks — kitty or puppy?**

   Kitty.

7. **Houses can be made out of logs. Why can't they be made out of sticks?**

   Because sticks would not be strong enough.

8. **If you were digging a hole, you might find rocks as you dug deeper, but you wouldn't find sticks. Why?**

   Sticks would decay in the earth.

9. **Since sticks are fun to play with, why don't stores sell them?**

   Because you can get them almost anywhere for free.

10. **Think of all the ways you might be able to use a stick.**

    To roast marshmallows or hotdogs; to make a ball bat; to make a fire; to stir something; to make marks in the dirt.

BIRD

1. How does a bird stay up in the air?

By flapping its wings.

2. How many things besides birds have wings?

Butterflies, moths, other insects, bats (which are mammals, not birds), airplanes.

3. Why do most birds have pointed beaks?

So they can pick up food easily.

4. Why are bird nests usually high up in trees?

Because that is where they are safest.

5. Why are most bird nests shaped like a bowl?

So that eggs will not roll out.

6. Why can you see birds better when they are flying than when they are on the ground?

Because the sky is a plain, light background. The ground is darker and has things like grass that can hide a bird. Also, rocks, leaves, etc. might look something like a bird.

7. Why do birds have such thin legs?

Because birds usually use their wings to get from one place to another. Also, thin legs are lightweight and make flying easier. (Exception: ostriches and other flightless birds, which have very strong legs.)

8. Where do birds go when it rains?

They usually sit in trees until the rain stops.

9. Why do birds sometimes look larger in the air than they do on the ground?

Because their wings and tail feathers are spread out when they fly.

10. Of all the birds you can think of, which is...
   — the largest?
   — the smallest?
   — the loudest?
   — the best flier?
   — the best swimmer?
   — the prettiest? (In your opinion.)

Answers will vary.

CITY

1. What is the biggest difference between a city and a town?

A city has more people.

2. Name three things you might see in a city that you wouldn't see in a town.

A skyscraper, a zoo, a large stadium, a subway, a parking garage, etc.

3. Why do you find tall buildings in a city?

Because they save space by stacking floors on top of each other.

4. Why are the streets in cities usually straight?

Because traffic flows more easily along straight streets. It is also easier to position buildings on straight streets and easier to find addresses.

5. During a power outage, where would you rather be — in a city or in a town? Why?

Answers will vary. Town is probably better due to fewer elevators, escalators, stop lights, big stores without windows, etc.

6. Why is it important to have parks in cities?

Because parks give people a place to play and to get away from man-made things.

7. **During what time of day, and during what days of the week, are there the most people in a city? Why?**

   During work hours (9-5) Monday through Friday, because many people who do not live in the city go there to work.

8. **The clerks in a big department store in a city probably wouldn't know your name. Why?**

   Because they see so many people every day.

9. **Many of the oldest, biggest cities are located by the ocean or by large rivers. Why?**

   Because water transportation was very important before the invention of trains, automobiles and airplanes.

10. **Do all towns end up being cities? Why or why not?**

    No, because towns don't always grow. (Because of location, distance from raw materials, area economy, population trends, etc.)

DOOR

1. Which two verbs, or action words, best describe what a door does?

Open, close.

2. About how many times a day do you go through a door?

Answers will vary.

3. Why are doors taller than they are wide?

Because that is the way people are shaped.

4. How many doors are there in your house or apartment?

Answers will vary.

5. When visitors come to your home, why do they knock at the door rather than at a window?

Because that is where they will enter the house.

6. Which doors in a house usually have locks on them?

Outside doors, bathroom doors, some bedroom doors.

7. Why do bathroom doors lock from the inside rather than from the outside?

For privacy.

8. Why is there a small space at the top and at the bottom of a door?

So the door will have room to open and close.

9. Why aren't door handles placed in the middle of doors?

Because they would be too hard to open.

10. What other things besides houses have doors?

Cars and trucks, buildings, airplanes, refrigerators, stoves, cabinets, etc.

PENNY

1. **Why are pennies made out of metal and not out of paper?**

   Because pennies change hands very often, would wear out, and would be more difficult to handle if they were made out of paper.

2. **If your mom or dad bought a car, why wouldn't they want to pay for it with pennies?**

   It would be hard to pay for a car with pennies because it would take too many.

3. **Why do people sometimes flip a coin such as a penny? Why not flip a button instead?**

   People flip coins to have a fair way of deciding between two things. Buttons wouldn't work because most of them are almost the same on both sides. Also, we seldom have one loose button available.

4. **Think of as many things as you can that are the color of a penny.**

   Autumn leaves, some kinds of wood, hair, syrup, some rocks.

5. **If you dropped a penny and a feather at the same time from the same height, which would hit the ground first? Why?**

   The penny. The air would keep the feather from falling as fast as the penny.

6. **Would a penny roll farther on a rug or on a gym floor? Why?**

   On a gym floor, because the surface is much smoother. (Less friction).

7. **Why don't you spend pennies at home?**

   Because the things we have in our house have already been paid for. They belong to us.

8. **What kind of store probably gets the most pennies — a furniture store, a restaurant or a candy store? Why?**

   A candy store, because the things sold there don't cost very much.

9. **Where do pennies come from?**

   They come from the government, which makes pennies in places called mints.

10. **Why aren't pennies made out of gold?**

    They would be too expensive and would no longer be worth just a penny.

SOCK

1. **Which would it be easier to put on in the dark — a pair of socks or a pair of shoes?**

   Socks. They have no left and right, and they don't need to be tied.

2. **Name three reasons why socks might be uncomfortable.**

   They might have a hole; they might not fit; the tops might fall down.

3. **Gloves have separate places for each finger. Why don't socks have separate places for each toe?**

   Because, unlike fingers, toes do not need to be used separately.

4. **Where do socks wear out the fastest?**

   In the heel or toe.

5. **Why doesn't your mother make your socks?**

   It would take too long. Besides, socks are not very expensive.

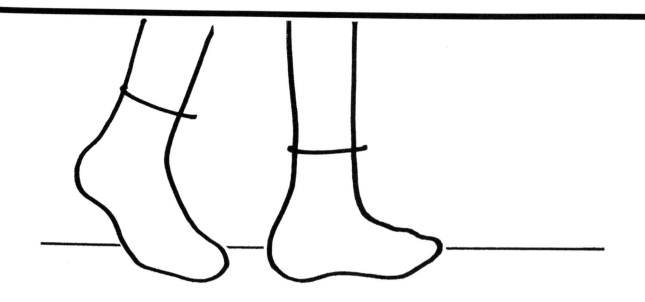

6. What is probably the most common color for socks? What would be the next most common color?

Probably white, followed by brown.

7. What would happen to your feet if you took a long walk wearing tennis shoes and no socks?

You would probably get some blisters.

8. Why don't socks get wrinkles in them?

They are made of material that tends to hold its shape.

9. What would be the advantage of buying six pairs of socks the same color? Would there be any disadvantages?

Advantage — it would always be easy to make up a matching pair; disadvantage — it might not be very interesting.

10. Describe every step you take when you put on your socks.

I take the socks out of the drawer, sit down on the bed, unroll the socks, put my toes in first, pull the sock over my heel, pull the sock up on my ankle, etc.

APPLE

1. Why do apples have seeds?

So they can make new apple trees.

2. Apples grow on trees. How many other things that we eat grow on trees?

Oranges, grapefruit, lemons, pears, plums, cherries, peaches, bananas, dates, olives, most nuts, etc.

3. The skin of an apple is very smooth. How many other foods have skins as smooth as the outside of an apple?

Plums, cherries, pears, grapes, perhaps bananas.

4. An orange often squirts you when you eat it. Why doesn't an apple do that?

It doesn't have as much juice.

5. If you wanted to cut an apple in half so that both halves were as closely alike as possible, would you cut it from the top to the bottom or around the middle?

From the top to the bottom.

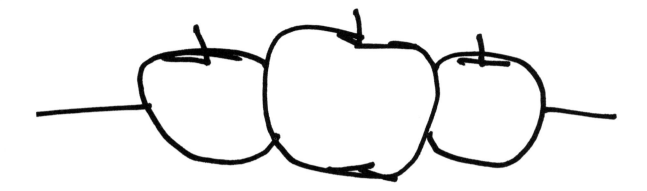

6. Name three ways in which the skin of an apple is different from the skin of an orange.

Apple skin is a different color, smoother, thinner.

7. What are all the steps people would have to go through to make applesauce?

Pick apples, peel skin and remove core, cook, mash, add seasoning, put in jars.

8. The number of apples needed to fill up a barrel depends on two main things. What are they?

The size of the apples and the size of the barrel.

9. Would it be easier to balance an orange on top of an apple or an apple on top of an orange? Why?

An orange on top of an apple, because apples have slight depressions at the top and the bottom.

10. Besides apples, how many things that we eat are one color on the outside and another color on the inside?

Bananas, potatoes, bread, eggs, coconuts, radishes, squash, watermelon, etc.

CAN

1. How do you tell what is inside a can?

By what the label says or shows.

2. In a grocery store, do you think there are more cans of food or boxes of food?

Probably cans of food.

3. Can you name one reason why a can is better than a jar? Can you name one reason a jar is better than a can?

Cans don't break. You can see what is inside of jars.

4. Think of eight foods that often come in cans.

Soup, soda pop, fruit juice, tuna, sardines, beans, tomatoes, chili, fruit cocktail, peaches.

5. How many things did you eat yesterday that you know came out of a can?

Answers will vary.

6. Which would probably stay fresh longer before you open it — something in a box or something in a can? Why?

Something in a can, because air can get through cardboard but not through the metal used in cans.

7. If you started with a row of five cans, how many more cans would you need to make a pyramid shape?

Ten.

8. In this world are there probably more...
  — soda cans or coffee cans?
  — spinach cans or green bean cans?
  — soup cans or juice cans?

Soda cans; green bean cans; soup cans.

9. What are some other things besides food that come in a can?

Oil, paint, tennis balls, bandages, cleansers, auto wax, shoe polish, etc.

10. How would a tin can roll differently than a ball?

The can would roll only frontwards or backwards. A ball would roll in any direction.

BICYCLE

1. Name as many parts of a bicycle as you can.

Wheel, rim, inner tube, tire, spokes, fenders, pedals, chain, frame, handlebars, seat, reflectors, etc.

2. How is learning to ride a bicycle something like learning to walk?

Both involve balancing.

3. What does a bicycle chain do?

It connects the pedals to the back wheel to make the bike go. (More accurately, it connects the large sprocket wheel by the pedals to the small sprocket wheel which forms part of the rear axle assembly.)

4. Could you ride a bicycle...
— without a seat?
— without handlebars?
— without a chain? (Discuss)

Without a seat — yes, you could stand up; without handlebars — probably not; without a chain — yes, but only when coasting.

5. If you turned your front wheel to one side and kept it that way while riding your bike, what pattern would you make?

A circle.

6. **What is the thinnest part on a bicycle? The highest part? The softest part?**

   Thinnest — probably spokes; highest — probably handlebars; softest — seat (or inner tube).

7. **What are some advantages of owning a bicycle rather than a car?**

   Less expensive to buy and operate; good exercise; no pollution; handy for short trips.

8. **Even though a bicycle has two wheels, it makes just one track in the dirt when going straight ahead. Why?**

   The rear wheel is directly behind the front wheel.

9. **One person is riding a big bicycle and one person is riding a small bicycle. Both are going the same speed. Would the wheels be turning faster on the big bike or the small bike?**

   On the small bike.

10. **How many different things can you name that have something to do with how fast a bicycle can go?**

    How fast you pedal; the road surface; the angle (up or down hill) of the road; the wind; the way the bike is made.

WATER

1. Water comes out of the sky in different forms. How many can you name?

Rain, mist, fog, snow, sleet, hail.

2. Name at least four different ways in which we use water.

To drink, to cook with, to clean with, to play in, to make things grow, to float boats.

3. Why do you think certain things float in water and certain things sink in water?

Because some things have more air in them than others.

4. When you stick your finger in water and it does not seem hot or cold, what temperature is it?

About the temperature of your body. (98.6 F)

5. Which usually flow faster — streams in mountains or streams on flat land?

Streams in mountains.

6. If you wanted to measure how many inches it might rain tonight, what could you do?

You could leave a glass with straight sides outside where it would catch rain, and then measure the amount of water you collect.

7. How do we get water from one place to another inside a house?

Through pipes.

8. When it rains, why do you often see puddles on the street but not in the grass?

Because water will usually soak into grass and dirt but not into pavement.

9. Do you think there is more water in an orange or a potato?

In an orange.

10. Name all the different ways in which you touch water during the day.

Answers will vary.

HAT

1. **Why don't people usually wear hats in their houses?**

   Many people think it is not polite. Also, hats are really not needed in the house.

2. **If you had to measure your head size, how could you do it?**

   You could wrap a tape measure around your head or use a string and measure the string with a ruler.

3. **What would be the most important reason for wearing a hat in a very hot climate? What would it look like?**

   For shade. The brim would be very wide.

4. **What would be the most important reason for wearing a hat in a very cold climate? How might it look?**

   To keep warm. It would be made out of something warm, like wool, and it would cover the ears.

5. **Many hats look different in the front than they do in the back. Why?**

   Because our faces need more protection than the backs of our heads. Also, we tend to put decorations on the front of things rather than on the back.

6. **If you look at the inside of a hat, what shape do you see? Why?**

   A circle, because our heads are shaped that way.

7. **Would it be easier to make a funny hat out of a head of lettuce, a pumpkin, or a loaf of bread? What's your opinion?**

   Answers will vary.

8. **Can you think of people in different jobs who almost always wear hats? Here's one: policeman.**

   Fireman, nurse, cook or chef, farmer, construction worker, sailor, baseball player, etc.

9. **A hat is to a person as a...**
   _____ is to a pan, and a
   _____ is to a house.

   Lid, roof.

10. **What other things do people wear on their heads besides hats?**

    Ear muffs, headphones, helmets, headbands, scarves, bows, hairpins, etc.

MAP

1. **Name five different kinds of things you might find on a world map.**

   Continents, oceans, large cities, large rivers, deserts, mountains, islands, etc.

2. **Name five different kinds of information a road map might give you.**

   Towns, roads, parks, distance between cities, highway numbers, etc.

3. **Why aren't schools and stores shown on road maps?**

   Because there are so many that there wouldn't be room for them all.

4. **Why don't school bus drivers use maps?**

   Because they know their way by heart.

5. **If you saw a long wiggly blue line on a map, what would it probably be?**

   A river.

6. Why are world maps put on the wall more often than road maps?

Because people often put world maps on the wall for decoration or to study them. Road maps are usually kept in the car so they will be there when we need them.

7. Do you think people in (name of your town) bought more road maps or world maps last year?

Probably more road maps.

8. Why do maps have to be changed from time to time?

Because the things that they show, such as roads, parks, etc., change from time to time.

9. Could a person in China and a person in (name of your town) use the same map of the world? Why or why not?

Yes, because even if the names of places are different in different languages, the places themselves are still the same.

10. If you had to make a map showing how to get from your house to school, what information would you have to include?

Direction, streets, important landmarks.

PET

1. Why do people keep pets?

Usually for enjoyment. Sometimes also for security.

2. What kinds of pets do people have?

Dogs, cats, birds, fish, turtles, hamsters, gerbils, rabbits, etc.

3. Why do more people have dogs and cats as pets rather than rabbits or turtles?

Because dogs and cats are smarter and easier to train.

4. Why do people pet dogs and cats from their heads to their backs?

Because that is the direction their fur grows.

5. Why do most dogs (and many cats) wear collars?

For identification, and so they can be put on a leash. (They also wear flea collars.)

6. What kind of pet would be the easiest to care for?

Answers will vary.

7. What do dogs do...
   — **when they are happy?**
   — **when they are afraid?**
   — **when they are angry?**
   — **when they are hungry?**

Happy — wag tail; afraid — bark, tail between legs; angry — bark, growl, hair on back stands up; hungry — bark, whine, beg or stand by food dish.

8. What do cats do...
   — **when they are happy?**
   — **when they are afraid?**
   — **when they are angry?**
   — **when they are hungry?**

Happy — purr, rub against your leg; afraid — arch back, run away; angry — hiss, arch back, hair stands up; hungry — meow.

9. Why do we name our pets?

So that we have a way to talk about them and to call them.

10. Could a ladybug be considered a pet? Why or why not?

Answers will vary. (A ladybug probably wouldn't make a good pet because we could not interact with it in any satisfying way.)

UMBRELLA

1. How many people do you usually see under an umbrella?

One.

2. If a father and his six-year-old child were sharing an umbrella, why wouldn't the child hold it?

Because the child would not be tall enough.

3. Besides height, what are some other reasons why it is hard to be under an umbrella when someone else is holding it?

Because umbrellas are fairly small. Also, people don't walk at the same rate of speed.

4. Which part of your body would probably get wet first when you're using an umbrella in the rain?

Probably your feet.

5. Think of two good reasons why dogs don't use umbrellas.

Because a dog could not hold an umbrella. Besides, dogs really don't mind getting wet.

6. Why don't children use umbrellas as often as adults?

Children often play and ride bikes in the rain, so raincoats are more suited to their activities.

7. Why are umbrellas hard to use in the wind?

Because of their shape, they catch the wind easily.

8. Why don't you use an umbrella when it is snowing?

Because snow usually doesn't get you very wet.

9. Can you think of times when you might take an umbrella with you even though it is not raining?

It might rain; if it is hot and sunny and you might need shade.

10. An umbrella is larger when it is used than when it is put away. How many other things can you name that are larger when they are used?

Tents, folding tables and chairs, ironing boards, beach balls, balloons.

COOKIE

1. **What is your favorite kind of cookie? Are there any kinds of cookies you don't like?**

   Answers will vary.

2. **What is it that makes a cookie a cookie? In other words, why isn't a potato chip a small cookie?**

   A cookie is usually sweet, small and flat.

3. **Why are most cookies sold at grocery stores perfectly round?**

   Because they are made by machines.

4. **Even though store cookies and home-baked cookies use about the same ingredients, store cookies usually cost more. Why do you think this is?**

   The people who make the cookies have to be paid. The people who own the store also have to make money when they sell the cookies.

5. **Home-baked cookies are almost always flat on one side. Why?**

   Because they are put onto cookie sheets while their dough is still soft. The part touching the cookie sheet stays flat, while the top part rises up as it bakes.

6. Why don't you butter cookies like you do bread?

Because cookies are rich enough already.

7. You eat cookies using just your hands. What other foods are eaten that way?

Many, including: fruit, sandwiches, potato chips, celery, carrot sticks, etc.

8. Why are most cookies a brown or tannish color?

Because they are slightly toasted as they bake.

9. Why are most chocolate chips still shaped like chocolate chips even after they are baked in cookies?

Because they are surrounded by cookie dough, which forces them to keep their shape while they are baking.

10. Cookie, a dessert, is a two-syllable word. Can you think of...
   — two desserts that have one syllable?
   — a sweet treat that has three syllables?
   — another treat that has four syllables?

One-syllable dessert — pie, cake; three-syllable treat — chocolate, marshmallows; four-syllable treat — watermelon.

KITE

1. **What is the most important thing you need to keep a kite up in the air?**

   Wind.

2. **Why are most kites made out of thin paper or plastic?**

   So they weigh less.

3. **Name all the things you would need to build a kite.**

   Thin paper, plastic or cloth; sticks, glue, string.

4. **Why don't people fly kites at night?**

   Because at night it would be hard to see them and to control them, and it wouldn't be much fun.

5. **Why would it be hard to fly a very tiny kite — say, about the size of your hand?**

   Because the kite would not be big enough to lift up the string.

6. **Why don't you use rope for flying a kite?**

   Because rope would be too heavy.

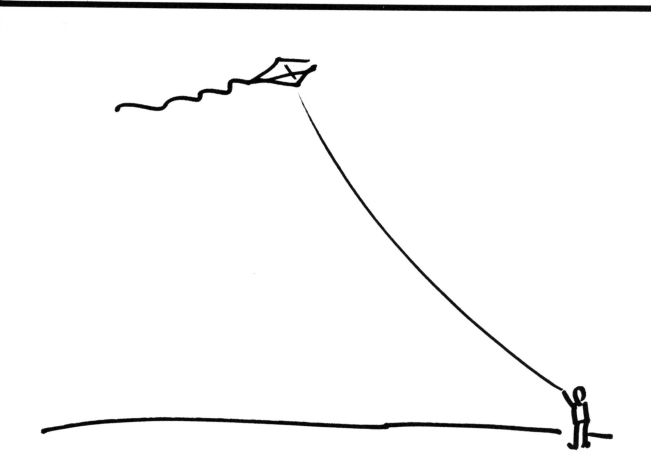

7. Think of at least two bad things which could happen to a kite.

The string could break; the paper could rip; the kite could get stuck in a tree.

8. Why aren't many kites colored light blue or grey?

Because kites of those colors would be hard to see against the sky.

9. Besides kites, what other things that you play with are in the air part of the time?

Model airplanes, balls, balloons, Frisbees, etc.

10. Besides kites, what other things must have wind to make them work?

Sailboats, windmills, some musical instruments.

CAR

1. **Why doesn't a car tip over when just one person is in the driver's seat all the way over on the left-hand side?**

   Because the four wheels of the car are a lot like the four legs of a table or chair, and things that rest on four legs (or wheels) don't tip easily.

2. **Cars can go forward and backward. Why can't they go sideways?**

   Their wheels won't turn that way.

3. **Why do cars have windshields?**

   To keep out wind, rain, snow, etc.; also, to protect the people inside from rocks, bugs, etc.

4. **Why are wipers needed only on the front, and sometimes the back, windows?**

   Because those are the windows that people most need to see through when they drive.

5. **Cars often have radios. Why don't they have television sets?**

   Because it is important for the driver to watch the road. Also, the passengers would probably get dizzy if they watched television in a moving car.

6. **The front seat of a car usually has more leg room than the back seat. Why?**

   Because the driver needs enough space to operate the pedals.

7. Why are a car's headlights down by the bumper rather than up near the roof?

This is a better position for lighting up the road. Also, it helps to keep the light out of the eyes of other drivers.

8. Cars have four wheels. Name some things which have one wheel, two wheels, three wheels, and four wheels. What things have more than four wheels?

One — unicycle, wheelbarrow; two — bicycle, motorcycle, some carts; three — tricycle, motorcycle with side car, light airplanes; four — light trucks, lawnmowers, some vacuum cleaners; more than four — large trucks, trains, large airplanes.

9. What are some advantages of taking a trip by car rather than by train or airplane?

Can take more luggage; can make any stops you wish; can decide own route; greater privacy; can make side trips after arrival.

10. Think of everything a car has that a house has.

Doors, windows, seats, heat source, sometimes air conditioning, roof, carpet, closets (glove compartment and trunk), radio, lights.

CLOCK

1. **How many clocks do you have in your house? Where are they?**

   Answers will vary.

2. **We divide time into seconds, minutes and hours. Why don't we use just hours?**

   We often need to be more exact.

3. **Clocks and watches keep track of time. Something else also helps us keep track of time. What is it?**

   Calendar.

4. **Do you look at a clock more often when you are at school or at home? Why?**

   Answers will vary.

5. **A school clock is usually larger than an alarm clock in your bedroom. Why?**

   It is made to be read from a distance.

6. **Which of these people probably would not wear a watch — a nurse, a train engineer, or a football player?**

   A football player.

7. **Think of two times when it might be important to use the second hand of a clock.**

   To time a race; to check heart rate; when cooking something where cooking time must be very exact.

8. **If all clocks and watches were digital, could you still use the phrases, "clockwise" and "counterclockwise?" Why or why not?**

   No. Because digital clocks do not have hands that go around in a circle.

9. **If you could have a clock with just a minute hand or just an hour hand, which would you choose? Why?**

   The hour hand, because you would always know about what time it was.

10. **Even if a clock is not working, it is still right how many times in a day?**

   Two.

NEWSPAPER

1. **The most important thing newspapers do is to print the news. What is "news?"**

   News is information about things that have happened that a large number of people want to know about.

2. **In what other ways besides newspapers do we learn about the news?**

   Television, radio, magazines, other people.

3. **Why are newspapers printed on paper that doesn't cost much money?**

   Because newspapers are usually printed daily in large numbers, read once, and then thrown away (or recycled).

4. **Why would a newspaper in a city have more pages than a newspaper in a town?**

   There are more things happening in a city. Therefore, there is more news to be printed.

5. **Why would you probably find more mistakes in a newspaper than in a book?**

   Because newspapers must be written and printed very quickly.

6. **The titles of newspaper stories are called headlines. Why do you think some headlines are larger than other headlines?**

   To tell us quickly which stories are most important.

7. **If the tallest building in your town or city had a fire, it would be in the newspaper. If you had a little fire in your garage, it might not be in the paper. Why?**

   Because a lot of people would be interested in the fire in the tall building, while only you and your friends and neighbors would care much about a little fire in your garage.

8. **Newspapers contain ads about things you can buy. Can you think of other ways you learn about things you can buy?**

   Commercials on television and radio, magazine ads, through the mail, billboards, word-of-mouth, etc.

9. **If a dog bites a person, it probably wouldn't be in the newspaper. If a person bites a dog, it might be in the newspaper. Why?**

   Because newspapers often contain stories about unusual things.

10. **What kinds of stories might be in a school newspaper? Use our school as an example.**

    Answers will vary. (Birthdays, lunch menus, school plays, sports, etc.)

HAIR

1. Why do people have hair on their heads?

Answers will vary. Warmth is probably best.

2. Name at least five things people do to make their hair look nice.

Comb, brush, wash, part, braid, cut, use bows, color, curl, etc.

3. Why do people get their hair cut?

For appearance; because hair that is too long can be a nuisance.

4. Why don't people cut their own hair?

Because they can't see the top and back of their heads, and scissors are hard to use while using a mirror.

5. It hurts when your hair is pulled but not when it is cut. Why?

There are nerve endings in the skin where hair is attached, but not in the hair itself.

6. Is one piece of hair thicker, thinner, or about the same as...
   — a thread?
   — a spider web?
   — a piece of string?
   — a cat's whisker?

Thread — thinner; web — thicker; string — thinner; cat's whisker — probably thinner.

7. If you took a test and missed an "A" "by a hair," what do you think that would mean?

You missed by just a little bit.

8. If the movie made "your hair stand on end," how would you be feeling?

Afraid.

9. How many ways are hair and fingernails somewhat alike?

They grow continually and need cutting; they have no feeling; they give some protection.

10. Can you name at least three ways hair gets messed up?

When we sleep; in the wind; when we wear a hat; when we swim (or shower); etc.

HANGER

1. Why do we need hangers?

So we can keep clothes from wrinkling; to save space by hanging many articles of clothing together in a closet. (Also, to keep clothes cleaner and more dust-free by storing them in a closet.)

2. Why don't we put socks on hangers?

Socks do not get very wrinkled and do not need to be hung up.

3. Who in your family probably uses the most hangers? Why?

Answers will vary.

4. Why are hangers curved at the top?

To fit over a closet pole.

5. Are hangers more the shape of a square, a triangle or a circle?

Triangle.

6. If you were camping in a tent, you probably wouldn't take hangers with you. Why?

It would be hard to find something to hang them on. Also, campers aren't very concerned about wrinkles.

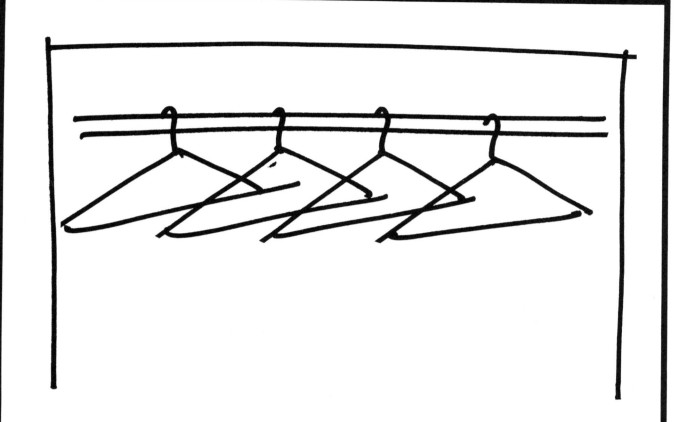

7. Hangers keep things neat. What other things do we use to keep things organized?

Drawers, shelves, tool boxes, sewing boxes, toy boxes, silverware trays, glove compartments in cars, wallets and purses, etc.

8. Why are hangers better than hooks for hanging up shirts?

Because a hanger is about the width of our shoulders and, unlike a hook, spreads a shirt out so it won't wrinkle much.

9. Why do you almost never see just one hanger by itself?

Because we need many hangers in order to store our clothes together in closets.

10. Besides hangers, what other things in your house come in groups and are about alike?

Spoons, table knives, forks, towels, paper clips, hairpins, sheets, pillowcases, etc.

CALENDAR

1. **If you were making your own calendar, how many sheets of paper would you probably use?**

   Twelve.

2. **Why is it important to have calendars?**

   Calendars give us a way to agree about when certain things will be done or will happen. They help us keep track of time.

3. **What is the next date on the calendar which is very important to you? Why?**

   Answers will vary.

4. **Thinking of calendars, explain the importance of the numbers 7 and 12.**

   Number of days in the week and months in the year.

5. **Finish this pattern with two more words: year, month…**

   Week, day.

6. Why do many calendars come with pretty pictures?

Because we often hang calendars on a wall or put them in other places where they can be seen easily. Therefore, we like them to look nice.

7. Why don't people carry calendars like they do watches?

Because the date stays the same all day, but the time always changes.

8. What is the most common ending for the names of the months — "er" or "ary?"

"Er."

9. Which month has the fewest letters?

May.

10. What is your favorite day of the week? What is your favorite month of the year? Why?

Answers will vary.

FLY

1. **During which season do you see flies the most often?**

   In the summer.

2. **Why do flies seem to be so much more of a bother inside the house than outside?**

   Because flies carry germs and we don't want them around our food. They are also simply a nuisance.

3. **Why do you see flies frequently in the kitchen?**

   Because flies are attracted to food.

4. **Do flies spend more time in the air or walking around? What's your opinion?**

   Answers will vary. "Walking around" is probably the better answer.

5. **Where would you find flies more often — on the floor or on a window?**

   On a window, because when flies are trapped in a house, they are attracted to the light of the outdoors.

6. **What are some of the methods we use to keep flies out of our houses?**

We use screens and keep unscreened doors and windows closed. We also swat flies or use fly paper. We keep garbage covered.

7. **Can you name a food which looks about the same color and size as a fly?**

A raisin. (Or a hamburger crumb or a chocolate chip.)

8. **Think about a fly's flying pattern. Does a fly move more in a straight line or in a circle?**

In a circle (especially indoors.)

9. **Flies are usually seen alone. Which of these other insects seem to be "loners" also? Bees, ants, mosquitoes, ladybugs.**

Ladybugs.

10. **Do you think a house fly weighs more or less than...**
    — a mosquito?
    — an earthworm?
    — a pea?

More than a mosquito; less than an earthworm or a pea.

FORK

1. Why don't very young children use forks?

Because forks are sharp and they might hurt themselves.

2. When you cut food on your plate, you use a knife, but you also use a fork. Why do you need the fork?

To hold the food in place while you cut it.

3. Why do people use metal forks more often than plastic forks?

They are stronger and can be used over and over again.

4. If you could have just a fork or just a spoon to eat with for all of next week, which would you choose? Why?

Answers will vary.

5. How is a fork like...
   — a comb?
   — a toaster?
   — a cup?

Comb — because both a comb and a fork have "teeth." (The "teeth" in a fork are called tines.); toaster — both are shiny, metal, and found in kitchens; cup — both are used when we eat and have handles.

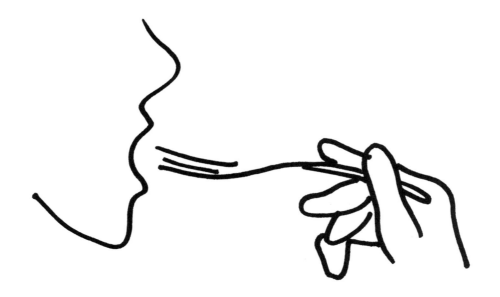

6. Is it easier to wash a fork or a spoon? Why?

A spoon, because a fork has several narrow places that are hard to wash.

7. If you drew a line all the way around a fork, a spoon and a knife, which line would be the longest?

The line around the fork.

8. What part of your body looks most like a fork? Why?

Your hand, because your fingers look something like the tines of a fork.

9. Why are peas hard to eat with a fork?

Because they are round and are hard to balance on the fork. They are also hard to stick with a fork because they are small and roll easily.

10. A fork has a handle. What other things found in the kitchen have handles?

Spoons, knives, cups, pots, pans, ovens, refrigerators, cabinets.

LIGHT

1. In your house, are there more ceiling lights or lamps?

Answers will vary.

2. What room in your house has the most lights?

Answers will vary.

3. Why is a lamp that sits on a table or on the floor sometimes better than a light on the ceiling?

Not as bright; shade can usually be adjusted to throw light on desired area; moveable.

4. Why are lamp shades usually white on the inside?

White reflects light the best.

5. What is the part of a lamp which wears out most often?

The bulb.

6. Are lamps in a house used more in the summer or the winter? Explain.

In the winter when the days are shorter.

7. Most ceiling lights are turned on by switches on the wall. What is the main reason why?

Convenience. So we will have light in the room before we enter it.

8. If there were no electric lights, what other light sources could be used?

Oil or kerosene lamps, candles, sunlight or moonlight.

9. If you wanted a little bit of light in your bedroom at night — but not much — what are a couple of things you could do?

Could use a night light; could turn on a light in another room and leave the door slightly open; could leave curtains open to let in outside light.

10. Speaking of lights, can you think of seven different kinds of lights you might see at night — not counting lights inside houses or buildings?

Star, moon, neon sign, street light, firefly, auto headlight, lightning, stoplight.

ROAD

1. **Do you think there were roads before there were cars? If so, what were they like and how were they used?**

   Yes. Roads then were narrow and unpaved. They were used by horse-drawn carts, wagons, and stagecoaches. Also, they were used by people riding horses and people walking.

2. **What are some reasons why the speed limit on some roads is lower than on others?**

   Some roads are narrow, and have many curves, hills, and cross-roads. It would be dangerous to go as fast on them as you would go on a big highway. Also, traffic has to move more slowly in cities and towns because there are more cars, intersections, people, school zones, etc.

3. **"Road" is one name for something we travel on. What is a common word for...**
   — **a big busy road between cities?**
   — **a road in a town?**
   — **a way from the road to your garage?**
   — **a way through the woods?**

   Between cities — interstate highway, highway, superhighway; in a town — street, avenue, boulevard; to your garage — driveway, perhaps alley; through the woods — path, trail.

4. **Roads are usually slightly higher in the middle than they are at the edges. Why do you think they are made this way?**

   So water will run off of them easily.

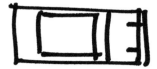

5. Why is litter usually found beside the road and not on it?

Since the road is smooth, there is nothing to catch and hold the litter. Also, passing cars make a breeze that blows it off the road.

6. Why might a small road be more interesting to travel on than a big interstate highway?

Because you would see more things.

7. One of these roads is in a city, one is in a town, and one is in the country. Which do you think is which?
— **Maple Street.**
— **State Route 87.**
— **129th Street.**

City — 129th Street; town — Maple Street; country — State Route 87.

8. Do you think it would cost more to build a mile of road through the mountains or through a desert? Why?

Probably through the mountains, because there would be steep places, large boulders, rock slides, canyons, mountain streams, etc.

9. Town "A" is ten miles away from town "B," but the road between the two towns is eleven miles long. What can you say for sure about the road?

It has some curves.

10. Can you drive on a road to every state in our country?

No. You can only reach Hawaii by plane or boat.

CHAIR

1. **Why don't chairs have just two legs?**

   Because they would fall over.

2. **What is the most common thing chairs are made of? Can you name some other materials often found in chairs?**

   Probably wood; other materials — metal, plastic, foam rubber, cloth.

3. **A family of six eats at a table in the dining room. How many chair legs are probably in the room?**

   24.

4. **Which is more important to you — having a chair with arms or a chair with a comfortable back? Why?**

   Answers will vary.

5. **In which room of your house would you find the heaviest chair?**

   Probably the living room.

6. **The seats of chairs are usually about the same height off the floor. What is the reason for this?**

   That is the most comfortable height for the average adult.

7. **Chairs have legs. What other kinds of furniture have legs?**

   Tables, chests, beds, sofas, stools, desks.

8. **Chairs could be much wider, but they couldn't be much narrower. Explain why.**

   If a chair is too wide, you can still sit in it. If it is too narrow, you would fall off or wouldn't fit.

9. **Think of your house. Are there more chairs than curtains? More chairs than tables? More chairs than rugs?**

   Answers will vary.

10. **How many hours in the day do you spend sitting in a chair?**

    Answers will vary.

KITCHEN

1. **Name everything in a kitchen that needs electricity.**

   Refrigerator, stove, microwave oven, toaster, mixer, blender, waffle iron, electric frying pan, dishwasher, clock, lights, etc.

2. **Why aren't kitchens carpeted like living rooms?**

   Because carpet would make it hard to clean up spills.

3. **Which drawer in your kitchen is used most often? Why?**

   Probably the silverware drawer, because we use knives, forks and spoons at almost every meal.

4. **Why is a clock important in a kitchen?**

   To time things that we cook. Also, the kitchen is a handy place to have a clock.

5. **Why don't kitchens usually have doors that open and close?**

   Because people carry things into and out of the kitchen very often and doors would get in the way.

6. **Why don't kitchens have floor lamps?**

   The kitchen floor area is usually small (to save steps) and floor lamps would get in the way.

7. **What (besides food) do you think are the three most important things in a kitchen?**

   Stove, refrigerator, sink.

8. Why do many kitchens have windows?

To let light in, to let fresh air in, and to make them more cheerful.

9. Think of six sounds you might hear in a kitchen. Here's one: the refrigerator running.

Water running, water boiling, mixer, timing buzzer, silverware rattling, bacon sizzling, dishwasher, refrigerator and oven doors closing, etc.

10. Think of your kitchen, and then name something in your kitchen which is...
   — white.
   — soft.
   — sharp.
   — metal.
   — tall.
   — heavy.
   — pointed.
   — shiny,
   — messy.
   — delicious.

Answers will vary.

FLAG

1. What is the purpose of a flag?

A flag stands for something — a state or a country, for example. (It is a symbol, in other words. We think of the thing it represents when we see it.)

2. Why does each country have a different flag?

Because each country is proud of what it stands for, and wants to have its own flag to show that it is different from all other countries.

3. Why do flags have simple shapes and bright colors?

So they can be recognized easily.

4. Why are flags the same on each side?

So they will look the same from any direction.

5. Why do people put flags up on tall poles?

So they can be seen easily by everyone.

6. Why do you almost never see a flag with writing on it?

Flags need to be simple so they can be recognized from far away. Also, so that people who do not speak the same language can recognize them easily.

7. Why don't people make flags out of paper?

They wouldn't last very long outdoors.

8. If you went to a city and saw a lot of American and English flags hanging together, what might be happening?

Someone important from England (like the queen) might be visiting.

9. Why don't countries change their flags every year or so?

For the same reason people don't change their names — flags stand for something important and lasting.

10. The things you see on a flag all stand for something. What do the 50 stars on the American Flag stand for?

The states.

CHALK

1. **Is chalk more like plastic, rock, or wood?**

   Rock. (Chalk is actually a form of limestone.)

2. **Why aren't pieces of chalk as long as new pencils?**

   Chalk is quite brittle and would break too easily if it were made into pieces that long.

3. **Why doesn't chalk come with an eraser on the end like a pencil has?**

   Because it takes a lot of chalk to make a mark and blackboards must be erased often. Therefore, a larger eraser is needed.

4. **Why doesn't the teacher use a tablet of paper and a pencil to explain something to students, rather than using a blackboard and chalk?**

   It would be hard for everyone to see what the teacher was doing.

5. **Why don't students write their assignments in chalk on little blackboards at their desks?**

   Paper and pencil are easier to use and don't make a mess. The assignments can also be handed in to the teacher.

6. **When you erase something which has been written on the blackboard, where do the chalk marks go?**

   Into the eraser. Also, some chalk dust stays on the board or drops into the tray.

7. Why is most chalk a light color?

Because blackboards are dark.

8. Why don't people use chalk on outdoor signs?

It would come off in the rain.

9. Name as many reasons as you can why it is harder to write neatly on a blackboard with chalk than it is to write neatly on paper with a pencil.

The blackboard is straight up and down; chalk smudges easily; and when you write on a blackboard, you must move your whole arm rather than just your forearm, wrist and fingers.

10. Which would make the longest mark before running out (if they were all the same length) — a piece of chalk, a crayon, or a pencil?

Probably the pencil.

GRASS

1. Why do people plant grass around their houses?

It looks nice; it also keeps the yard from becoming muddy or dusty.

2. Why do people mow their grass?

To make it look better. It is also easier to walk on and play on if it is mowed.

3. What things in nature are needed for grass to grow well?

Sunlight, water, good soil.

4. What games are played on grass?

Football, baseball, soccer, croquet, badminton, etc.

5. If you were walking barefoot in the grass, what hidden things might hurt your feet?

Thistles, bees, glass, sticks, rocks, etc.

6. Why is it hard to see a grasshopper in the grass?

It is small, and it is often the color of grass.

7. Why aren't roads made out of grass?

The grass would wear down too easily.

8. Why doesn't a piece of grass bend over when an ant walks on it?

The ant is not heavy enough to bend it.

9. Is a piece of grass more like a spoon, a fork, or a knife?

A knife. In fact, a piece of grass is called a blade.

10. Name three things which might be found...
  — under the grass.
  — in the grass.
  — over the grass.

Under — worm, rock, dirt; in — twig, ant, drop of water; over — bird, tree, sky.

STAMP

1. **When you receive a letter in the mail, the stamp on the envelope has some black lines through it. Why do you think these lines are there?**

   The post office puts them there to show that the stamp has been used. (This is called canceling the stamp.)

2. **Why do stamps have to be in the same place on the envelope each time?**

   So it will be easier for the post office to make sure the letter has a stamp on it, and then to cancel the stamp.

3. **Besides a stamp, what else has to be on the front of an envelope before you mail it?**

   The name and address of the person the letter is for. (It is also a good idea to put your own address on the envelope.)

4. **To get a letter ready to mail, you have to lick a stamp and put it on the envelope. What else has to be licked before you mail a letter? Why?**

   The flap on the envelope, to keep the letter private and to keep it from falling out.

5. **When you buy a stamp and put it on an envelope, what are you really paying for?**

   You are paying the post office to deliver the letter.

6. Why do stamps have bumpy edges?

Because they come attached to one another and have to be ripped apart before they are used.

7. Why wouldn't it be a good idea simply to put a stamp on your letter and forget about the envelope?

Without an envelope, the letter could get torn in the mail. Also, everyone could read it.

8. Why don't people save the money used to buy stamps and just give people their letters?

Because they would often have to travel long distances to give people their letters, and the trip would cost much more money than the price of the stamp.

9. Who uses the most stamps in your family? Why?

Answers will vary.

10. Some people collect stamps. Why would stamps be a good thing to collect?

Stamps are colorful and fun to look at, easy to store, and do not cost much.

Index

Other Publications by Tin Man Press

Is It Friday Already? Learning Centers That Work — A year's worth of learning center ideas in nine subject areas.

The Great Unbored Bulletin Board Book — 20 challenging bulletin board ideas you've never seen before.

The Great Unbored Bulletin Board Book II — Who says sequels can't be equal? This one is. 20 more original boards.

The Great Unbored Blackboard Book — Uses the blackboard as a focus for lively thinking activities.

Waiting for Lunch — Serves up quick, easy, mostly oral activities to do with your class when you have an extra few minutes.

OPQ — Offbeat Adventures with the Alphabet — The alphabet becomes the springboard for all sorts of intellectual play.

Linework — A 64-card set designed to give children varied and unusual experiences with the concept of line.

An Alphabet You've Never Met — This 64-card set asks students to think of words suggested by some creative tampering with letters.

Discover! — A series of 24 card sets which use everyday objects for a hands-on approach to thinking skills. 20 challenges per set.